BIG-TIME BUSINESS

SOCIAL NETWORKING
BIG BUSINESS ON YOUR COMPUTER

Nick Hunter

W
FRANKLIN WATTS
LONDON • SYDNEY

Franklin Watts
First published in Great Britain in 2015 by The Watts Publishing Group

Produced by Calcium

Acknowledgements:
The publisher would like to thank the following for permission to reproduce photographs: Cover:
Dreamstime: Hongqi Zhang cl; Shutterstock: Veronika Rumko cl, Valdis Torms cr, Takayuki cr. Inside:
Paul Clark: 8cr; Devin Cook: 6bl; Dreamstime: Jacek Chabraszewski 29tr, Danieloizo 10b, Gruffydd
Thomas 32b, Marcellofar 28br, Vlue 9b, Wrangler 3, 44b; Istockphoto: Sherwin McGehee 23r;
Guillaume Paumier: 40cl; Spotify: 36br; Shutterstock: Yuri Arcurs 21br, A Turner 19cr, Carme Balcells
19tr, Radu Bercan 35t, Bullet74 42bl, Cinemafestival 17tr, Conrado 31tr, Cristovao 19tcr, Djem 13tr,
Elena Elisseeva 19tcmr, 38bl, Helga Esteb 24cl, Goodluz 37br, Richard Griffin 13br, Jorg Hackemann
19cmrr, Christopher Halloran 25tr, Holbox 19bmr, Blend Images 12r, Monkey Business Images 14b,
15t, Kenjito 33cl, Layland Masuda 19tmr, Miks 20–21c, Photobank.kiev.ua 30r, Pistolseven 4cl, Omer
N Raja 45br, RoxyFer 16t, Annette Shaff 18b, Rui Vale de Sousa 19tcmrr, Jason Stitt 34br, Konstantin
Sutyagin 19tmrr, SVLuma 4bl, Takayuki 22cr, Pit Tan 43t, Testing 39b, Liviu Toader 7br, Kiselev Andrey
Valerevich 27br, Wavebreakmedia ltd 5l, 1000 Words 41t, Andy Z. 7l; Yahoo: 10t; You Tube: 25tr.

Dewey number 338.4'7006754
ISBN 978 1 4451 3923 4

Printed in China

Franklin Watts
An imprint of
Hachette Children's Group
Part of The Watts Publishing Group
Carmelite House
50 Victoria Embankment
London EC4Y 0DZ

An Hachette UK Company
www.hachette.co.uk

www.franklinwatts.co.uk

CONTENTS

LIFE ONLINE

The Internet has changed the way we live. We can use it to plan days out in our local area or a holiday on the other side of the world. We can shop online or sell things we no longer need. The Internet has also changed the way we communicate with each other.

Online takes over

The change began when we started sending emails rather than just phoning someone or meeting face to face. People found it easier to communicate quickly by instant messaging and online chatrooms. Since 2000, hundreds of millions of people have joined social networks.

Online, people can now meet, talk and share photos, music and every detail of their lives.

4

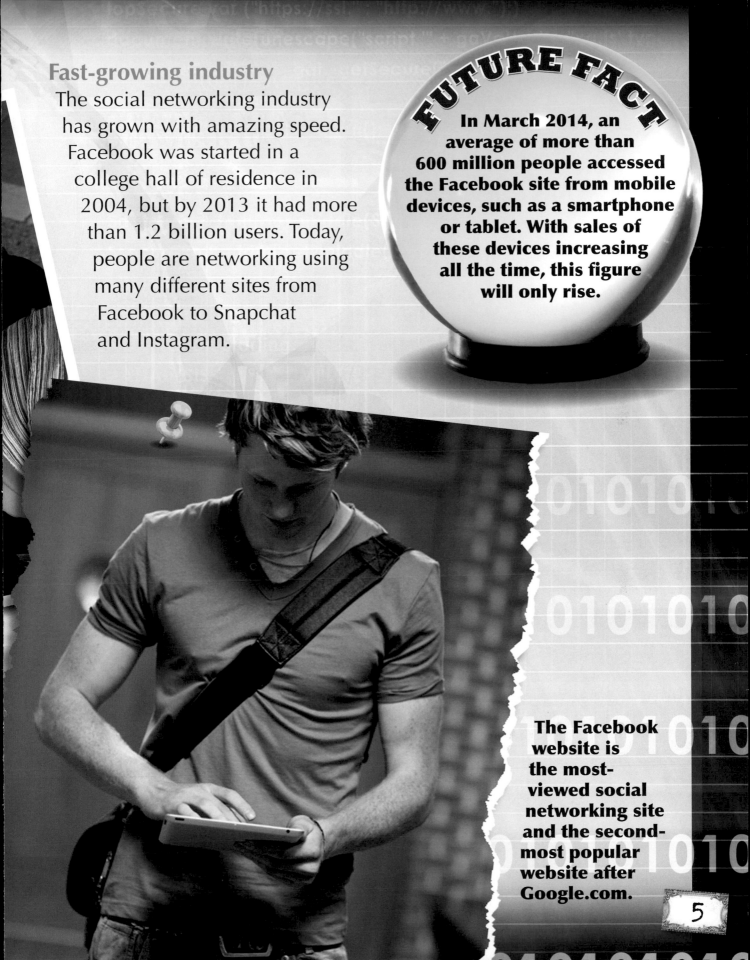

Fast-growing industry

The social networking industry has grown with amazing speed. Facebook was started in a college hall of residence in 2004, but by 2013 it had more than 1.2 billion users. Today, people are networking using many different sites from Facebook to Snapchat and Instagram.

FUTURE FACT

In March 2014, an average of more than 600 million people accessed the Facebook site from mobile devices, such as a smartphone or tablet. With sales of these devices increasing all the time, this figure will only rise.

The Facebook website is the most-viewed social networking site and the second-most popular website after Google.com.

CHAPTER 1

HOME COMPUTERS

The Internet has brought dramatic changes.
An office, school or home in the 1980s would have
had one or more personal computers (PCs), but they
were basic and difficult to use compared with today's
technology. They were mostly used by people with
a special interest in computing or word processing.

The arrival of PCs

In the late 1970s, businesses
such as Apple and software
company Microsoft started to
make PCs and programs that
ordinary people could use.
They were not very powerful by
today's standards, but people
began buying them for use at
home and at work.

**During the
1980s, computer
companies improved
the look of PCs and
made them more
user-friendly.**

Linking up

In 1990, most home and business computers could share information with other computers only if they were connected by a network cable. This all changed with the launch of the World Wide Web.

Many of the computer industry's pioneers were based in an area of California called Silicon Valley.

WORLD'S RICHEST PERSON

The people who launched the personal computer industry in California's Silicon Valley made a great deal of money. Bill Gates, founder and creator of Microsoft, became the world's richest person. Gates has used much of his wealth to fight poverty and disease around the world.

BIRTH OF THE INTERNET

The Internet was first developed in the 1960s. It allowed computer users in different government and research locations to link their computers to each other so that they could exchange information. Tim Berners-Lee, a British scientist at CERN, invented the World Wide Web (WWW) in 1989. The web was originally designed to allow automatic information sharing between scientists in universities and institutes around the world. In 1993, the US government allowed non-government users to access the Internet to share information and the World Wide Web was made available to the public.

Tim Berners-Lee developed the software behind the World Wide Web as a way for scientists to exchange reports.

Information superhighway

Businesses soon worked out that they could make money from the 'information superhighway', as the World Wide Web was known in the 1990s. Internet service providers (ISPs) gave users access to the Web and email. Other companies developed software that helped users to browse the Web.

Making the Web work for business

The first websites were mostly information providers. Yahoo! started as a list of recommended websites. It grew to include a search engine, information on business and other topics, and services such as email. Yahoo! and AOL (America Online) tried to attract as many users as possible by offering free information and services.

Traditional postal services have suffered because we send more communications by email than through the post.

THE FIRST 'DOTCOM' BOOM

By the late 1990s, millions of people were using the World Wide Web. New businesses were set up to make money from online customers. One of the biggest was Amazon, which began by selling books and then other products. Internet traffic grew rapidly, people started using email and every business had to have a website.

Amazon was started by Jeff Bezos in 1994. It has become one of the world's biggest retailers.

Online businesses multiply

Investors soon realised that online companies were worth investing in. Online stores could reach customers all over the world, and other companies could reach the same people by advertising on the stores' websites.

Dotcoms

Investors rushed to put money into companies that added '.com' to their name. Most of the companies in the dotcom boom of the 1990s were online versions of traditional shops and businesses. The boom in the value of dotcom businesses reached its peak in 2000.

BUST!

At their peak, dotcom businesses were considered to be worth millions, even though their sales came to little more than those of a small shop. When investors realised that many would never make money, the value of dotcom shares fell sharply and many companies went bust.

11

WEB 2.0

From 2000, more
and more people became
Internet users. Faster
Internet connections replaced
slow dial-up connections.
This meant that Web users
could download larger audio
and video files from the Web.
Users could also upload their
own photos and videos to
share with friends.

Your words and pictures

A new type of online business, known
as Web 2.0, developed. The businesses
relied on customers to provide the
words, pictures and other features of
their websites. Examples of Web 2.0
include social networking sites, blogs,
wikis and video-sharing sites.

**In the United States alone, the
world's biggest music market,
sales of CDs dropped from
138 million CDs in 2009 to
just 65 million CDs in 2014.**

The social Web

Users soon discovered that through the Web they could connect to old and new friends in a 'social network'. More and more people signed up to sites such as Myspace and Facebook. If their friends were on one of these sites, they had to be, too!

Changing music

The music industry changed greatly as people began to listen to and share music online. Since 2010, CD sales have been in huge decline with more and more people choosing to download music rather than buy it in physical form.

FUTURE FACT

Many retail businesses, such as travel agencies and bookshops, have moved their business online and closed their high street shops. In the future, more industries, such as advertising, are likely to be affected by the success of social networks.

Affordable technology enables ordinary people to make and upload their own films.

CHAPTER 2

WHAT IS A SOCIAL NETWORK?

A social network is a website that people use to connect to, and communicate with, friends. People mainly use social networks to share photos and talk online. They also use them to arrange parties or reunions, or even promote a business.

Previous generations only socialised face to face. More and more people today are using social networking to make friends.

Why do people belong to social networks?

People join social networks because they like to make connections or friendships. A social network allows us to keep in touch with people, no matter how little or often we see them. It allows us to share our interests and find out more about our friends.

FUTURE FACT

We use social networks to write articles or upload our own music. Today, fewer budding journalists bother to try to get their work accepted by newspapers or magazines. Will the Internet completely replace CDs and printed literature in the future?

Many people stay in touch with their friends throughout the day via social networking sites. Communication through social networks is usually free.

Networks need people

Customers are essential for any business and this is also true of social networks. Without customers, social networks could not make money, so they try to attract as many people as possible.

FIND YOUR FRIENDS

One of the first social networks was classmates.com. It was launched in the United States in 1995 and put people in touch with old friends from school or university. SixDegrees.com, which launched in 1997, was the first social network to connect different groups of friends. Friends Reunited is a popular site that reunites friends who have lost touch with each other. The site was launched in the United Kingdom in 2000.

Simple social networks

Early social networks struggled to make the profits they needed to survive. They were very simple and did not have all the features that today's social networks provide. Customers did not expect to pay for their services, and online advertising was still developing.

Social networks such as Myspace helped young bands to share their music with fans.

16

Friendster

After 2000, things changed very quickly. Friendster, a social networking site, was launched. It became popular with users in technology and software industries. It was soon overtaken, however, by the network called Myspace.

Rupert Murdoch recognised the importance of social networking for the future of his vast media business.

Myspace

Myspace was launched in 2003, and it was a different kind of social network. Users could customise their profile pages and upload music and other media. Myspace allowed users to express themselves. The company was bought by Rupert Murdoch's giant media company, News Corporation or News Corp, in 2005 for £360 million. By 2006, it was the most visited website in the United States but since then has lost value as users switched to Twitter and Facebook.

FACEBOOK EFFECT

A rival social network to Myspace appeared in 2004.

Student Mark Zuckerberg started 'the facebook' as a way for students at Harvard University to connect with each other. It grew rapidly and began to pick up new users by the millions. In 2006, Facebook became available to users around the world. By the end of 2013, Facebook had more than 1.2 billion users.

Facebook profiles

Setting up a profile on Facebook is very simple. Once set up, users can add applications and features to make their profile as complex as they want. This has made Facebook popular with everyone, from grandmothers to school students.

From 2006, anyone over the age of 13 with an email address could have their own Facebook profile.

Heading out? Stay connected
Visit facebook.com on your mobile phone.

Facebook grows

As Facebook became more popular, Myspace declined. Facebook provides users with more ways to connect and share things online. For example, it has linked to the music service Spotify, so users can see what their friends are listening to.

Controversies

Facebook has come under criticism with complaints that it does not do enough to protect against online bullying. Some say that it allows customers who use the site to advertise their business too much access to private information about users.

FUTURE FACT

The more time people spend on Facebook, the more Facebook finds out about its users. It can use this information to sell advertising and make money in other ways.

People from every generation and many different social backgrounds use Facebook.

CHAPTER 3

A WORLD OF SOCIAL NETWORKS

Facebook is the biggest social network, but it has many competitors. A lot of other online businesses want some of the success that Facebook has had.

For many people, online social networks are as important as the social network provided by their local community.

TAKE CARE WHAT YOU SHARE

Personal information is used by social media companies to make money. However, it may also be used by criminals. This means it is very important to be careful what personal information you share and who you share it with.

Fighting Facebook

Some social networks deliberately do things differently from Facebook in order to attract users. Google+ was launched by the Internet giant Google, which dominates the business of online searching and advertising. Users of Google+ can create separate groups of friends, such as school friends or family. They can then share different things with their individual groups.

Filling a need

Some social networks try to satisfy particular groups of users. LinkedIn, for example, helps business people to make and share contacts and has added features such as job postings. Other social networks are popular in particular places. Qzone, for example, created in 2005, is the biggest social network in China.

Making connections with other business people is important in many industries.

THE BLOGOSPHERE

Blogs are often linked to social network websites. They range from respected pieces of writing on specialist subjects to a person's thoughts about what they did that day. If you sign up to a blog, you are told by email when the next installment of the blog is available to read.

All kinds of blog

There are millions of blogs on the Web on every subject, from music to politics. Many are personal notes, while others are written to support a business. Some blogs advertise related businesses that may be of interest to their readers.

Blogs enable people to share their interests or knowledge with people all over the world.

A question of trust

Blogs and social networks both provide an alternative to traditional media, such as newspapers and television. They are successful because people enjoy being updated with information and suggestions or tips from people they trust. However, there is a downside to the information available on a blog – it may simply be the views of the author and contain little fact or substance. Unlike blogs, newspaper articles have usually been carefully researched to make sure the information they contain is accurate.

FUTURE FACT

Between 2004 and 2014 sales of Sunday newspapers in the United Kingdom fell by nearly 48 per cent. In order to keep their readers, many newspapers now offer their information online as well as in print, and more are likely to do so in the future.

Reading the news in a printed newspaper may one day be a thing of the past.

23

TWITTER AND OTHER MICROBLOGS

Celebrities such as Justin Bieber can talk directly to their millions of followers on Twitter.

A microblog is similar to a blog but has much less information. The best-known microblog service is Twitter, which was started in 2006 by Evan Williams, Biz Stone and Jack Dorsey. Twitter users can send short messages, called tweets, to their followers and follow tweets posted by other users. Many celebrities and businesses use microblogs.

A good business?

Being able to reach a community of customers is valuable for many businesses. Twitter has more than 250 million users, but some people question whether microblogging businesses will be able to make money from their users. Twitter itself makes a sizeable amount of its money through selling advertising space. At least 85 per cent of its revenue comes from advertising.

On location

Smartphones have made the Internet mobile. People use them to connect to the Internet when they are out and about. This has led to the creation of location-based social networking sites, such as foursquare.com. Users can register their location while on the move, and local advertisers can then sell products to them.

USEFUL FOR BUSINESS

Social networks are important tools for businesses. By attracting friends and followers on social networks, businesses can create communities of customers, who they can target with advertising and offers. They may also get useful feedback and ideas from their customers.

Barack Obama was one of the first politicians to realise the importance of social networks in winning an election.

1010101010101

SHARING VIDEOS AND MUSIC

Sharing music and videos is an important part of social networking. If sites such as Facebook can persuade people to watch videos on their website, customers will spend more time on the site.

In 2006, YouTube was bought by Google for £940 million.

Video king

YouTube is the biggest video platform on the Web. Users upload their personal videos to YouTube, and viewers watch the videos online or share them via a social network. Like many social networking sites, users can visit YouTube without paying anything.

Super growth

YouTube was started in 2005. By the summer of 2006, it was already hosting 25 million videos. By 2010, the company could boast that 24 hours of new video were uploaded every minute!

The site makes its money through selling advertising to its clients, who want to promote their products and businesses to the millions of people who use YouTube for free. YouTube made the decision to offer free viewing and use in order to create an audience of millions – and thereby attract vast numbers of businesses that pay YouTube to advertise them.

Worth billions

By 2008, the company had a projected revenue of £127 million, thanks to its advertising sales. Today, the business is said to be worth a staggering £25 billion!

According to one survey, people who listen to streamed music are less likely to share music files illegally.

FUTURE FACT

People can now stream music and videos. They no longer need to download the files, which saves them money. Artists and film-makers are losing out as a result. Without the money from downloads, they will find it harder to produce new work in the future.

GAMING

The computer revolution brought with it computer games. The first online games appeared in the late 1990s. As broadband Internet connections got faster, the gaming industry boomed. By 2013, Microsoft's Xbox Live network had 46 million users.

Multi-player online games

One of the most popular online games is World of Warcraft. Players compete against each other, or work together in groups, to complete tasks. They can 'chat', or talk, online to other players, making the game a social experience.

At the end of 2013, World of Warcraft had 7.8 million paying players.

Unlike most social networks, many online games charge a monthly fee to gamers.

Online games and social networks

Games have become a key part of social networks, especially Facebook. The games CityVille, FarmVille and Candy Crush Saga have millions of users. Social networks try to offer their users everything they want from the Web, without having to go outside their social network.

CHAPTER 4
MAKING MONEY FROM SOCIAL NETWORKS

A great bonus of social networking is that it is free. You can create a Facebook profile or start using Twitter without paying anything. This has helped the biggest social networks to attract huge numbers of users.

Costing money

A social network has to pay for offices, computer programmers and lots of computers and servers to store all the photos and other information that users want to share. So how does it make enough money to pay these expenses? Most of its money comes from selling advertising and credits for online games.

Social network entrepreneurs can make millions from investors if their networks can attract enough users.

Users are happy to sign up to a social network that keeps them in touch with friends, as long as they do not have to pay.

FUTURE FACT

Facebook had sales of £4.6 billion in 2013, which amounts to nearly £4 per user. This is much less than is made by Apple and Google. Investors expect Facebook's sales to grow enormously in the years to come.

Keeping it free

The most successful social networks know that the more users they have, the more opportunities they have to sell advertising. If the networks started charging for their services, their users would probably sign up with a free, rival network instead.

ONLINE ADVERTISING

Social networks use advertising to make money. Internet advertising can be aimed much more closely at the right people than television or radio commercials.

Social networks can provide advertisers, such as Apple, with valuable, detailed information about possible customers.

Targeting the market

Advertisers try to target their advertisements at people who are most likely to buy their products. Google has been very successful at linking advertising with the searches people make for specific words on their search engine.

How much do you reveal?

Do you have a social network profile? Think about all the things that the company providing the service knows about you from your profile. It knows your age, where you live and what businesses or celebrities you follow. The more information you share online, the more useful you are to the social network because it can target you with advertising that fits your profile.

Every time you click on an advertisement, it tells social networking businesses a little more about you.

FUTURE FACT

In 2013, £6.3 billion was spent on online advertising in the United Kingdom – an overall increase of more than 15 per cent on 2012. $13.9 billion was spent on online advertising in Australia in 2013.

THE VALUE OF DATA

What is the main product that a social network has to sell?

It is not the service itself, because that is free. The main product is you! The network provider collects all the data it can about you and passes that information onto advertisers. Advertisers can then filter the information to find their target market, for example, teenagers, to ensure that well-aimed adverts pop up on their Facebook pages.

Businesses, recruiters and colleges and universities can find out about you from social networks. Take care what you share!

The personal touch

If you are looking for a good place to eat out, you might do an online search, but you are just as likely to ask a friend to recommend somewhere. A business such as a restaurant will advertise 'special offers' online to attract customers. It hopes the customers will then recommend it online to their friends.

Who benefits?

Advertisers use the data they get from social networks to target products at people. Businesses use data to design new products that they think people will want to buy in the future.

Personal recommendations on social networks are a great way for businesses to attract new customers.

PRIVACY

Many people are happy to give up some of their privacy for the benefits that a social network brings. Other people believe that customers should be given more information about how their personal data is being used.

THE FREEMIUM

Social networks can make money by charging customers for special services. Networks that do this are called 'freemium' businesses. The idea is that most customers can use the service for free, but a small number of users who use the service a lot, or who want to use special features, have to pay. The paying customers cover the costs of the service and ensure the network makes money.

More for your money

Social networks that offer freemium services know that only a small number of their many users are likely to pay for the special freemium services. The business network LinkedIn offers paying customers greater access to the millions of business people who use the network. It is a valuable service to people who want to make new contacts.

Spotify

Buying credits

Facebook makes money by selling credits that are used in online games. Only a small number of its users pay for these, but Facebook has so many users that this adds up to hundreds of millions of pounds.

Spotify's users can listen to music without paying but will be targeted by advertisers, or pay a monthly fee to listen advert-free.

Companies pay social networks to access the data provided by customers who use their freemium services. The data is used by salespeople to sell products.

37

CHAPTER 5
THE BIG PLAYERS

Social networking is still a very young industry. The world's biggest social networks have been running only since 2000. Many have not yet made a profit because the costs of attracting and providing a service to millions of users are so high.

Big money

Google has invested a lot of money in social networks and media, including Google+ and YouTube. As a result, Google has made big money from advertising. In fact, its online advertising business provides 97 per cent of the company's total revenue.

Companies that advertise on social networking sites can attract huge sales of their products.

Facebook adds features

Although Google makes large profits from social networks, it offers fewer services than the biggest social networks. Facebook dominates the industry and continues to add new features to hold the interest of its users. Twitter also became popular by offering a different kind of social network.

Google has tried to compete with Facebook by linking social networking to its other services, such as its search engine.

39

SOCIAL NETWORK BILLIONAIRES

The biggest players in social networking are said to be worth hundreds of millions or even billions of pounds. How did they get to be so rich, when many of the social networking businesses they run do not yet make a profit?

The face of Facebook

The most famous figure in the world of social networking is Mark Zuckerberg, the founder of Facebook. In 2014, Zuckerberg was said to be worth more than £17.5 billion – at the age of just 30. This is based on the value of Facebook as a business if Zuckerberg decided to sell it. In 2010, *Time* magazine named Zuckerberg as its Person of the Year, pointing out that if all Facebook's users were in one country, it would be the third biggest country in the world!

Mark Zuckerberg of Facebook has been learning Chinese so that he does not miss out on a billion possible customers.

+You

Social networking is just part of Google's giant technology business.

Search engine stars
Larry Page and Sergey Brin founded Google, the most popular search engine on the Web. Google makes billions from online advertising. The Google+ social network is probably the biggest threat to Facebook.

Biggest bloggers
Biz Stone and Evan Williams founded the blogging service Blogger.com in 1999. Not content with that, they went on to found Twitter with Jack Dorsey. Twitter is said to be worth billions of pounds.

FUNDING THE BOOM

The biggest players in social networking were all still in their twenties when they had ideas that would change the world. To make their ideas reality, they needed money.

Taking a risk

Venture capitalists are people who put money into new businesses. They will give money to a new business in exchange for owning part of the company. It is a risky thing to do because many new companies do not survive and very few achieve the sort of success that Facebook has had. In fact, 90 per cent of all Internet start up businesses fail!

Venture capitalists can provide the money that social networks need to become global players.

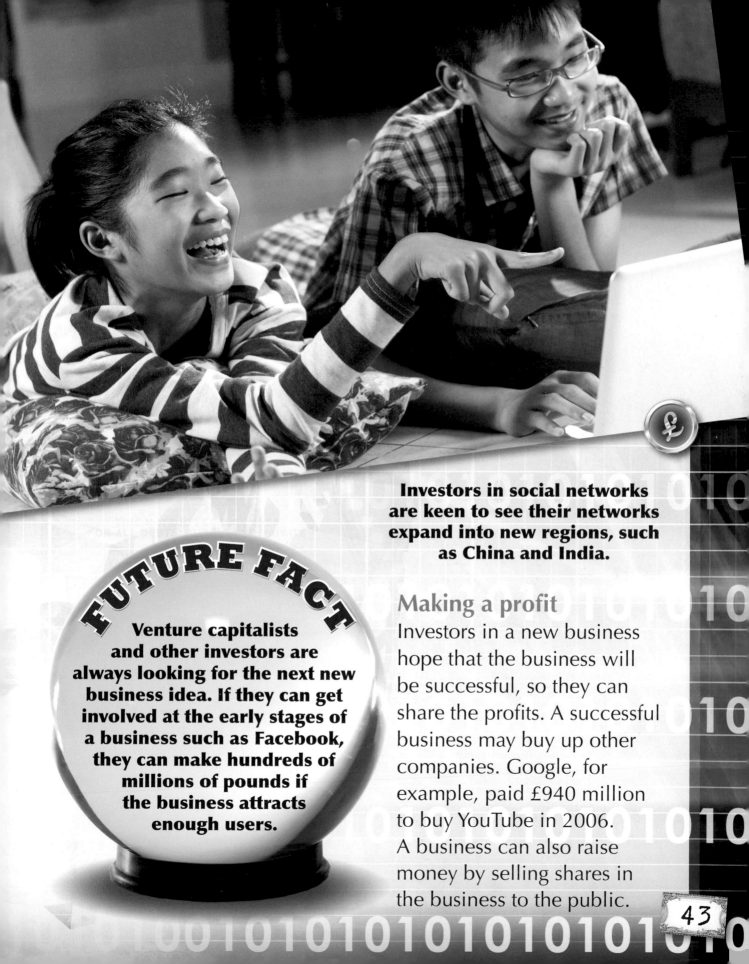

Investors in social networks are keen to see their networks expand into new regions, such as China and India.

Making a profit

Investors in a new business hope that the business will be successful, so they can share the profits. A successful business may buy up other companies. Google, for example, paid £940 million to buy YouTube in 2006. A business can also raise money by selling shares in the business to the public.

FUTURE FACT

Venture capitalists and other investors are always looking for the next new business idea. If they can get involved at the early stages of a business such as Facebook, they can make hundreds of millions of pounds if the business attracts enough users.

43

CHALLENGES
AHEAD

In less than a decade, social networks have become a huge part of our lives. We already use Facebook and other networks for communication, leisure and gaming, and the big players in the industry would like us to use their networks even more.

Making money

The biggest challenge for social networks is turning their millions of users into profits through advertising. Will people be happy if their profile pages are cluttered with adverts, or if they have to pay for features that were once free? Social networks think they will be.

Almost half of all users now visit social networks through their phones.

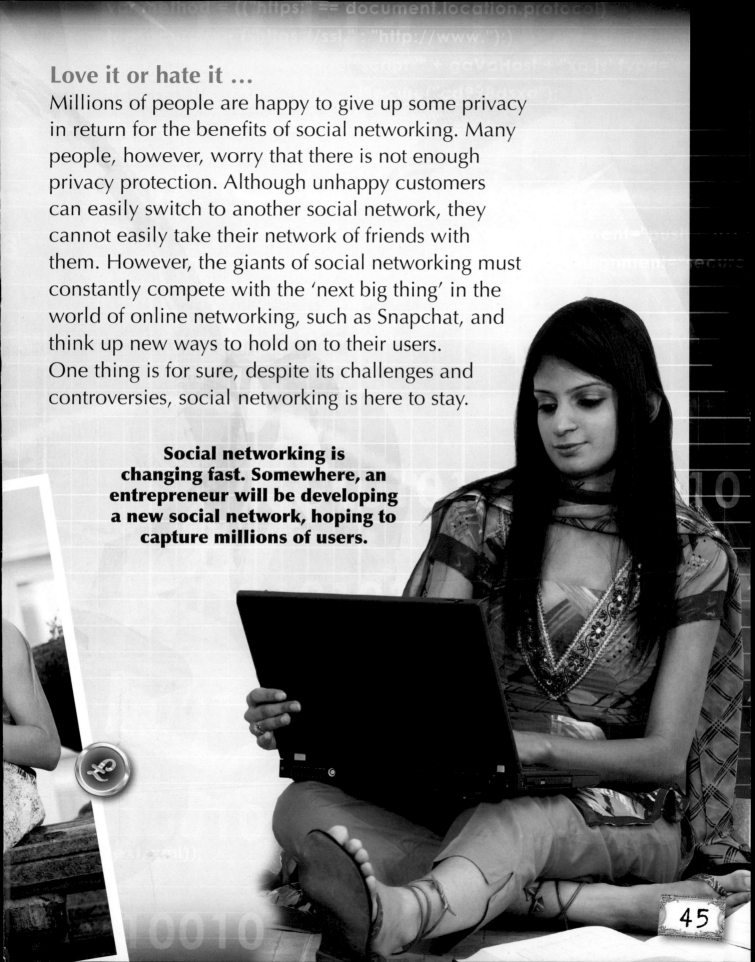

Love it or hate it …

Millions of people are happy to give up some privacy in return for the benefits of social networking. Many people, however, worry that there is not enough privacy protection. Although unhappy customers can easily switch to another social network, they cannot easily take their network of friends with them. However, the giants of social networking must constantly compete with the 'next big thing' in the world of online networking, such as Snapchat, and think up new ways to hold on to their users. One thing is for sure, despite its challenges and controversies, social networking is here to stay.

Social networking is changing fast. Somewhere, an entrepreneur will be developing a new social network, hoping to capture millions of users.

GLOSSARY

blogs short for web logs, which are diaries or logs that people can store on a website and update regularly

broadband a high-speed Internet connection that enables users to access video and other services online

browse process of viewing or clicking between different websites

chatrooms online services that let users communicate with instant messages

credits tokens or electronic vouchers that can be used online instead of money

currency a form of money, such as Australian dollars or Japanese yen

customise change to suit the needs of a particular user

data information held on a computer

dial-up connections slow Internet connections made by dialling a phone number

emails messages that are sent electronically via the Internet

hosting providing a 'place' on the Internet for a website

Internet connections links between computers and the Internet. They connect computers to millions of other computers

Internet service providers (ISPs) companies that provide computer users with an Internet connection

Internet traffic the flow of data across the Internet

messaging creating and exchanging short messages, such as emails, using a computer

network cable a cable that connects a computer to a network of other computers. Computers connected by a wireless connection do not need a network cable

platform an operating system on which a program or device runs

posted put on the Internet

profile pages the personal pages for users on a social network and the information they contain

profits money that a business makes on top of the money it has spent or invested

search engine a computer program that searches documents for a specific word and supplies a list of the documents where that word was found

shares parts of a company that can be bought or sold on a stock market

smartphone a mobile phone that can connect to the Internet and run other applications

stream send video or audio files in a continuous stream of data, which the user plays as it arrives, live over the Internet

upload transfer a file from a personal computer to the Internet so it can be viewed by others

venture capitalists people who raise money to invest in companies

wiki a website or document that many users can add data to or edit

46

FOR MORE INFORMATION

BOOKS

Facebook (Big Business), Adam Sutherland, Wayland

Social Networks and Blogs (Mastering Media), Lori Hile, Raintree

The Quick Expert's Guide to Social Networking, Anita Naik, Wayland

The Story of Facebook (Built for Success), Sarah Gilbert, Franklin Watts

WEBSITES

Find out more about social networking at:

www.netsmartz.org/TeensTalkBack/SocialNetworking

www.facebook.com/zuck

You can also discover more about social networking on social networking websites themselves, such as Twitter or Google+. Look for sections with headings such as 'about this site' or 'company info'.

Note to parents and teachers
Every effort has been made by the Publisher to ensure that these websites contain no inappropriate or offensive material. However, because of the nature of the Internet, it is impossible to guarantee that the contents of these sites will not be altered. We strongly advise that Internet access is supervised by a responsible adult.

INDEX